The AI Democratization

How Small Businesses Can Leverage It

Table of Contents

Chapter 1. Introduction

Welcome to our latest Special Report, "The AI Democratization: How Small Businesses Can Leverage It." In an era where technology can often feel overwhelming, fear not! This timely piece is designed specifically with you - innovative but perhaps technically wary small business owners - in mind. We've stripped away the jargon, ensuring the substance is accessible to everyone – even those without a background in computer science! Unpack the burgeoning world of AI and uncover practical strategies to harness its power, irrespective of your business's size or industry. Inspiration awaits just a few clicks ahead; let's embark on this exciting AI journey together to unlock immense potential and profits! Dive into this report. You're just one step away from transforming your business with AI!

Chapter 2. Understanding AI: An Intro for Small Businesses

Before we delve into the practicalities of leveraging AI, it's instrumental for small business owners to develop a foundational understanding of what AI is and what it's not. Artificial Intelligence, or AI, has been an object of fascination and a theme of science fiction for decades. Fast forward to today, it's no longer just a figment of our imaginations but an integral part of our daily lives and an emerging toolkit for businesses, big or small.

AI is a broad concept that encompasses many subfields, including but not limited to, Machine Learning (ML), Natural Language Processing (NLP), Robotics, and Computer Vision. What all these fields share in common is the aspiration to mimic, supplement, or surpass human intelligence and capabilities using computational frameworks.

2.1. AI vs. Human Intelligence

We humans, by nature, are intelligent beings, capable of understanding, learning, reasoning, and adapting. Over millions of years, we've evolved an intricate neuronal network – the brain – which allows us to process information, make decisions, and interact with our environment.

AI researchers, inspired by the biological brain, aim to create machines capable of 'intelligent behavior.' Here, 'intelligent behavior' refers to the capability of a machine to understand its surroundings, learn from experiences, adapt new strategies based on the learnt knowledge, and perform tasks that would require human intelligence.

While there's a long way to go before machines fully replicate human consciousness or emotions, they can often exceed human capabilities in narrowly defined tasks, provided they're trained with sufficient data.

2.2. Clustering the AI: Different Types

There are three generally recognized types of AI:

1. Narrow AI: Refers to AI that excels at performing a single task, such as recommending songs, detecting spam emails, or playing chess. These systems can sometimes surpass human performance but only within their specific task. Examples include Google Search, Siri, and most commercially available AI today.

2. General AI: These systems have a broader range of capabilities and can perform any intellectual task a human can. They can understand, learn, adapt, and implement knowledge across a range of tasks. Today, this kind of AI is still purely theoretical, with no practical models or examples in use.

3. Superintelligent AI: If an AI system ever surpasses humans at most economically valuable work, it would be known as 'superintelligent.' This concept, though not achieved yet, is widely discussed in the realm of futurology and makes for compelling themes in science fiction.

For small business owners, the focus will primarily be on Narrow AI and its application in the form of machine learning.

2.3. What Is Machine Learning (ML)?

Machine Learning (ML) is a popular subset of AI aiming at providing machines the ability to learn and improve from experience without being explicitly programmed. The purpose of ML is to enable machines to automatically learn and improve from experience by feeding them with vast amounts of data and letting them adjust and improve by identifying patterns and making data-driven predictions or decisions.

There are three main types of ML: supervised learning (where models are trained on a labeled dataset), unsupervised learning (where algorithms find patterns and relationships in unlabeled data), and reinforcement learning (where an agent learns to behave in an environment, by performing actions and seeing the results).

The choice among these depends on the task at hand and data available. Algorithms used in these include – but not limited to - linear regression, decision trees, clustering algorithms like K-means, and neural networks.

2.4. Demystifying Deep Learning

Deep Learning is an even more specialized subset of ML involving artificial neural networks with several ("deep") layers. This kind of AI learns to identify patterns in layers of data – much like our brain neurons do. This technique is behind several "magical" tech feats like image recognition, voice recognition, natural language processing, and autonomous vehicles.

2.5. Practical AI Applications for Small Businesses

Now that we understand the basics of AI and its various forms let's talk about its practical applications for small businesses. Just because you're not running a tech-savvy company doesn't mean AI can't help you. Here are a few examples:

1. Personalized Marketing: AI can analyze customers' behavior and spending patterns and make recommendations, enhancing

customer experience and boosting sales.

2. Customer Support: AI chatbots can provide round-the-clock customer support, answering basic queries and relieving your human employees for more complex requests.

3. Forecasting: Predictive algorithms can forecast sales trends, helping in inventory management.

4. Cybersecurity: AI and ML can recognize suspicious activity and raise alerts in real-time, securing your digital assets from cyber threats.

With a better understanding of what AI and its subsets are, and the value they can bring, in the next chapters, we will delve deeper into how you can implement AI into your business - irrespective of your technical background or skillset. We aim to demystify AI and enable you to leverage it for commercial advantage, operational efficiency, and enhanced customer experience. So, buckle up as we navigate through the exciting world of AI for small businesses!

Chapter 3. Busting AI Myths: Debunking Common Misconceptions

Artificial intelligence (AI) has increasingly become part of our daily lives, influencing decision-making in a diverse set of industries, from healthcare to finance, retail to education. But, like any other game-changing technology, it isn't exempt from skepticism, misconceptions, and hearsay. It's time to confront those myths and debunk them with facts to better understand and leverage AI for your small business.

3.1. The Complexity Myth

Many believe that AI is complex and only feasible for larger corporations with deep pockets and extensive technical teams. This is far from the truth. Today, numerous AI tools can be easily implemented with little to no coding skills. Affordable plug-and-play solutions exist that allow even start-ups to benefit from AI. For instance, customer service chatbots, predictive analysis tools, and marketing automation, are increasingly within every business's reach.

3.2. The Job Terminator Myth

It's a common misconception that AI adoption implies job losses, as machines would replace humans. Yet, the reality presents a different picture. AI and automation have the potential to augment human capabilities, not just replace them. They can carry out repetitive, mundane tasks, freeing humans to focus on higher-value tasks which demand creativity, critical thinking, and complex problem-solving skills.

3.3. The Expense Myth

AI can seem expensive, with the perception that it's a technology restricted to companies with vast financial resources. But, considering the plethora of SAAS-based AI tools available in the market, AI implementation can be surprisingly affordable. Various open-source tools also exist, which can be customized to suit specific business needs. The most important expense is the willingness to learn and adapt, demonstrating the true democratized nature of AI.

3.4. The Data Privacy Myth

There is anxiety about AI contributing to breaches in data privacy. While it is accurate that AI systems require data to function efficiently, strong security measures and privacy-preserving methodologies like differential privacy and federated learning can ensure your data remains secure. It's crucial to vet AI vendors thoroughly, ensuring they follow stringent data protection norms.

3.5. The Perfect System Myth

A myth that often weighs on the decision-makers is the belief that AI is infallible. However, AI systems are designed by humans and run on data generated by humans, making them susceptible to mistakes, biases, and inaccuracies. Emphasizing the importance of transparency, rigorous testing, and continuous refinement is essential to mitigate any adverse effects.

3.6. The Self-Learning Myth

Another misconception is that all AI systems are self-learning, automatically improving with time. While some advanced AI systems can learn and improve, not all possess this capability. AI is just a tool and needs guidance and supervision from human experts for improvement and optimal performance over time.

3.7. The AI-Necessity Myth

Lastly, businesses often perceive that they need to adopt AI to stay competitive. While AI offers valuable benefits, it should align with the business's strategic goals and solve specific problems. Merely adopting AI for the sake of technology without a clear use-case would be neither profitable nor ideal.

AI has the potential to transform every aspect of your business. By debunking these myths, we hope to encourage its adoption and more informed decision-making. It's time to harness the power of AI, driving your business's growth and profitability.

Chapter 4. AI and Your Business: Identifying Opportunities

Artificial Intelligence (AI) is not merely about fantasy movie scenarios and sleek robots anymore - it is an integral part of our everyday lives. From personalized Netflix recommendations to chatbots providing customer service around the clock, machine learning applications are everywhere.

But what does this mean for your small business? How can you exploit this powerful technology to solve operating challenges and carve out a competitive edge?

This chapter is here to demystify AI for you. We won't train you to be a data scientist - that's not our aim. Instead, we want to empower you to think strategically about AI, understanding how you can harness it with your current resources.

4.1. Understanding AI and its Potential for Small Businesses

Before we proceed, it's crucial to understand what AI truly encompasses. Artificial intelligence is essentially programming computers and machines to mimic human intelligence. It's a broad field, containing several subdomains like Machine Learning (ML), Natural Language Processing (NLP), Robotics, and more.

Small businesses may feel daunted by the prospect of using AI. However, it's less about creating an advanced AI from scratch and more about leveraging existing AI technologies to suit your needs.

The potential of AI lies in its ability to spot patterns in massive data sets that would take humans ages to analyze. This can lead to valuable insights that can significantly improve and streamline your business operations.

4.2. Identifying Opportunities for AI in Your Business

To uncover how AI can be beneficial for your business, you must audit your current operations and identify areas where AI can be integrated. Here are a few steps to get you started:

1. Evaluate Your Operational Bottlenecks: Start by understanding your operational pain points. Is it slow customer service response times? Or perhaps inefficiency in scheduling deliveries? By identifying these areas, you define problems that AI can potentially solve.

2. Understand Your Data: AI thrives on data. This data could range from your customer's buying behaviour to your website's analytics. Understanding the kind of data you already have is critical to determining how AI can help.

3. Seek Inspiration from Others: Keep an eye on how similar businesses in your industry are utilizing AI. This can provide a plethora of information and inspiration.

4.3. AI Applications and Your Business

Now that we've touched on how to identify AI opportunities for your business, let's explore some common AI applications that are easier to adopt and highly beneficial for small businesses.

1. Customer Service Chatbots: Chatbots can engage with customers

around the clock, providing immediate responses and reducing the burden on human customer service teams. AI-driven chatbots can learn from each interaction, becoming more competent with time.

2. AI-Enhanced Analytics: With AI, you can analyze huge data sets in real-time. This allows you to gain valuable insights about your customers, competitors, and industry trends far quicker than manual analysis.

3. Predictive Analysis: AI can analyze historical data and predict future trends. In industries like retail, this might mean predicting which products will sell during a particular season. This allows for a more efficient stock management, avoiding both overstock and outages.

4. Personalization: AI can tailor user experiences leveraging data about a user's habits and preferences. It can lead to increased customer engagement and satisfaction.

Remember, the idea is not to understand each technical nuance, but to understand what is possible. Consider how each of these AI applications might solve your business challenges or improve your current practices.

4.4. Making AI a Reality for Your Business

Leveraging AI does not necessarily demand a significant financial input. Tools like Google Cloud AutoML, Microsoft's Azure AI, and AWS's SageMaker put AI at the disposal of small businesses. These, combined with data you already own, can lead to powerful business solutions.

Identifying the right synergies between these tools, your data, and business needs is crucial. It may require professional guidance, but with clear problem definitions, the cost of implementation can be minimized and the process made more efficient.

Remember, AI is a journey. Start small, learn, evolve, and gradually upscale. A modest beginning, such as implementing chatbots on your website, can yield substantial returns over time.

The possibilities AI presents to small businesses are immense. It's a cutting-edge technology not to be feared, but understood and utilized. Your journey into AI does not have to be a leap in the dark; with proper strategy, understanding, and gradual integration, it can be a systematic drive towards better competitiveness and efficiency.

Chapter 5. The Economics of AI: Cost-Benefit Analysis for Small Businesses

Artificial Intelligence (AI) is no longer confined to the world of science fiction and large technology-led enterprises. Today, it spreads across various industries and size of businesses, becoming an essential part of our daily lives and altering the economic landscape. Now let's explore various aspects of AI economics to grasp its value proposition better for small businesses.

5.1. Initial Investment and Ongoing Costs

The economics of AI usually begins with understanding the initial investment and ongoing costs. These expenses primarily include software development, licensing, hardware, maintenance, and upgrade costs which can vary significantly depending on the AI solution you adopt.

In-house AI development can be costly for small businesses mainly due to the need for specialized skills and resources. It requires technically proficient staff with expertise in AI and machine learning. Implementing AI solutions also require powerful hardware, which can lead to significant investments.

On the other hand, leveraging third-party AI services or platforms can often be a more cost-effective choice for small businesses. Numerous providers offer AI as a Service (AIaaS), which allows companies to utilize AI capabilities without developing the software in-house. Cloud-based AI solutions and Software as a Service (SaaS) can drastically reduce the technology costs while providing the ability to scale easily as per business needs.

However, it's essential to consider potential ongoing costs such as subscription fees, expenditures on regular updates, and system maintenance. Technical support, data storage, and security are also crucial costs that businesses need to factor in.

5.2. Assessing ROI: Anticipated Benefits and Savings

Understanding the potential return on investment (ROI) in AI is as crucial as defining the costs. The primary benefits derive from automating processes, enhancing productivity, delivering unique insights through data analysis, and creating superior customer experiences.

AI can automate repetitive and mundane tasks, allowing staff to focus more on strategic, creative, and decision-making aspects of the business. This shift towards high-value tasks can lead to tangible productivity enhancement, which translates into cost savings and higher income.

Another significant benefit of AI comes from leveraging data. AI-driven analytics can reveal in-depth insights about customer behavior, market trends, and operational efficiency, which can drive strategic decisions leading to enhanced competitiveness, increased sales, and improved profitability.

AI can also enhance customer experience by providing personalized service and support. Intelligent chatbots, for instance, can engage customers, answer queries, and provide support 24/7. These innovations can lead to improved customer satisfaction, loyalty, and ultimately, increased sales.

However, keep in mind that these benefits might not be immediate.

There's usually a lead-time between implementing AI and realizing its full potential as users must learn and adapt to the new systems and processes.

5.3. Cost-Benefit Analysis Example: Implementing an AI-based Chatbot

Let's consider a specific example of implementing an AI-based chatbot for customer support to illustrate a cost-benefit analysis.

The initial costs might include the purchase and integration of a chatbot into your system offered by a third-party AIaaS provider. Assuming this costs $2000 per annum. Depending on your specific needs, necessary customization, ongoing system maintenance, and upgrades could add an additional $500 per year. So, the total annual cost is $2500.

On the benefits side, assuming that previously, a team of two customer service representatives working full-time handled customer inquiries. If you pay each representative $30,000 per annum, the total cost is $60,000. If the AI-based chatbot can handle 80% of the inquiries, you can significantly reduce these labor costs.

Additionally, improved customer service efficiency, reduction in response time, and resolution rate could lead to an estimated increase in sales by 5%, which in a business generating $500,000 in annual sales, equates to an additional $25,000.

By comparing the costs and benefits, you can evaluate the ROI. Be aware that the actual numbers will vary drastically based on your unique circumstances, and this is simply to illustrate the concept.

5.4. Ethical, Legal, and Social Considerations

While weighing the economic benefits of AI, small businesses should not overlook the ethical, legal, and social considerations. AI decision-making models, for example, could inadvertently introduce bias, leading to potentially discriminatory practices. Businesses could also face legal implications tied to privacy and data security issues. Considering these aspects is imperative to mitigate future risks and unintended consequences that could potentially lead to reputational harm or financial loss.

5.5. Future Proofing Your Investment

As technology evolves, so does AI. Ensuring that your AI investment is future-proof is essential. Fortunately, cloud-based AIaaS models can typically facilitate this due to their inherent design for scalability and regular updates. Moreover, investing in personnel training and development to better leverage AI tools also aids in future-proofing your investment.

In conclusion, while AI does represent an investment, its transformative potential can greatly benefit small businesses. From automating processes to garnering deep insights from data, the economics of AI offers a competitive advantage. It's not about replacing human resources but redirecting them to areas where they can bring more value. As with any significant business decision, however, the decision to adopt AI should follow a careful cost-benefit analysis that considers both immediate needs and future growth.

Chapter 6. Starting Small with AI: Micro-implementations

AI is not an endpoint, but a journey. It can seem daunting for small businesses to tackle, as it often comes with the idea that it requires extensive investment, resources, and highly skilled professionals. However, the reality is significantly different. The fundamental idea behind 'Starting Small with AI' is to understand that you don't have to be an AI giant right from the start. You can begin with humble, smaller steps referred to as micro-implementations. These are modest, manageable applications of AI that steadily impact business outcomes and can be built upon over time.

6.1. Understanding Micro-Implementations

Micro-implementations are small scale implementations of AI, designed to be low-risk but high impact. These are steps that even smaller businesses can take to start leveraging AI power without needing massive resources or specialized knowledge. They concentrate on solving specific issues or optimizing a particular process within an organization.

A micro-implementation approach focuses on targeted applications of AI—one problem, one solution. It could include automating repetitive and mundane tasks, something as simple as a chatbot handling routine customer queries, or using predictive analytics to improve inventory management. In essence, a micro-implementation targets a 'small' problem, creating an opportunity for 'big' improvements.

6.2. The First Steps to AI: Identifying Areas of Application

Before venturing into specific micro-implementations, it's vital to identify potential areas within your business operations where AI could help. This should start with assessing your business needs, evaluating your current resources, and understanding what technology adoption would mean for your operations.

Ask fundamental questions like:

- Where is your business bottlenecked?

- Which processes could improve from automation?

- Where could predictive analytics drive more effective decision-making?

- What simple, repetitive tasks could be handled by AI, freeing up your staff for more complex roles?

This initial analysis helps figure out the most feasible and beneficial areas for your business to implement AI.

6.3. Micro-Implementation Examples: Real-World Applications

To help illustrate the concept of micro-implementations, we have gathered a few examples of small AI applications that have been used by businesses globally to improve their operations in tangible ways.

6.3.1. Chatbots and Virtual Assistants

Chatbots have seen immense growth in recent years. Serving as a virtual assistant, these pieces of AI can handle common customer inquiries, thus freeing up time for service representatives to handle more complicated cases.

6.3.2. Predictive Analysis for Inventory Management

Retail businesses, e-commerce, and wholesalers often struggle with maintaining a balance between excess and insufficient inventory. Through predictive analysis, a retailer can more accurately forecast demand, reducing instances of overstocking or running out of products.

6.3.3. Data Analysis and Insights

AI tools can also help analyze business data more efficiently and in real-time. Through machine learning algorithms, they can detect patterns and trends that manual analysis may overlook or take too long to uncover.

6.4. Implementation: Starting Your AI Journey

Once you have identified your needs and opportunities, the real work begins. Micro-implementations, though small, require careful planning and implementation. Here are some steps to guide you:

6.4.1. Assessing your Resources

What skills do your employees already possess? What technology is already at your disposal? What data do you already attract and store?

6.4.2. Building a Team

Depending on the complexity of your project, you may need to develop an AI team. This doesn't necessarily mean hiring new staff; you could upskill current employees or collaborate with a third-party provider.

6.4.3. Planning the Project

Start by setting a clear goal for your AI application. This should be tied to a specific business challenge identified earlier. Use this goal to plan your project, defining timelines, allocating resources, and assessing potential risks.

6.4.4. Executing the Project

Start with a pilot project, testing your chosen AI solution on a small scale before fully implementing it. This enables to you measure the impacts and if necessary, make adjustments before the full roll-out.

6.5. Scaling up: Going Beyond Micro

Remember, the ultimate goal is not to stay small. As you familiarize yourself with AI's workings and learn how to integrate it into your business processes, you can start thinking bigger. Each micro-implementation can serve as a stepping stone towards more extensive, complex AI projects.

Whether your future AI applications involve advanced data analytics, autonomous systems, or AI-driven innovation, start with the small, manageable steps that micro-implementations offer. This approach makes AI accessible, allowing even small businesses to gradually tap into its immense benefits. Remember, every AI giant started with a single, humble step.

Chapter 7. AI Tools: An Overview of Accessible Resources

As technology expands, a growing number of Artificial Intelligence (AI) tools have become accessible to streamline processes and improve business outcomes. Many of these tools require no coding, making them a perfect fit for small businesses that might not have a dedicated tech team.

7.1. Understanding AI Tools

AI tools include any type of hardware or software technology that incorporates AI algorithms to automate certain actions. These tools can perform a wide array of tasks, from data analysis and forecasting to automating customer interactions and marketing efforts.

AI tools can transform small businesses by making operations more efficient and effective. This is done through automating tasks, gathering actionable insights from business data, improving customer service, and fostering innovation.

7.2. Types of AI Tools

AI tools come in diverse forms, each catering to different areas of small business operations:

1. **AI Chatbots**: AI chatbots are virtual assistants that can simulate conversations with users. They can be used for customer service, lead generation, and to provide answers to frequently asked questions. Examples include: Drift, LivePerson, and MobileMonkey.

2. **Marketing Automation Tools**: Using AI, these tools can optimize marketing campaigns based on data analysis. They personalize customer messages and track marketing performance. Some examples are HubSpot, Marketo, and Pardot.

3. **Sales Forecasting Tools**: Sales forecasting tools use predictive analytics to forecast sales trends. This can help businesses to plan better and make informed decisions. Examples include Salesforce Einstein, Zoho CRM, and Clari.

4. **Business Intelligence Tools**: These tools gather, analyze, and interpret data into actionable insights to help businesses make strategic decisions. Examples include Tableau, QlikView, and Looker.

5. **Process Automation Tools**: By automating repetitive tasks, these tools can save small businesses significant time and resources. Tools such as UiPath, Automation Anywhere, and BluePrism are popular examples.

7.3. Benefits of AI Tools

For small businesses, the core benefits of AI tools are time-saving, cost-efficiency, and yielding higher-quality outputs.

1. **Increased Efficiency**: AI tools can automate repetitive tasks and processes, allowing staff to focus on higher-level activities.

2. **Cost Savings**: By automating tasks, businesses can reduce labor costs and direct resources toward more critical areas.

3. **Improved Decision Making**: AI tools can analyze large volumes of data, providing meaningful insights that aid in strategic decision-making.

4. **Enhanced Customer Experience**: AI tools can improve customer interactions through personalization and automation, leading to improved customer service.

7.4. Choosing the Right AI Tools

The selection of AI tools should be driven by your specific business needs. There are a few main considerations:

1. **Identify the Need**: The first step is identifying what tasks could be improved by AI automation.

2. **Budget**: Understanding your spending limit for AI tools is key. They range from free to enterprise-level fees.

3. **Usability**: An AI tool should be user-friendly and require minimal training to implement.

4. **Scalability**: As your business grows, your AI tools should be able to handle increased usage and complexity.

5. **Vendor Support**: Good vendor support is essential to solve any technical issues that may arise.

7.5. AI Tools: Overcoming Challenges

While AI tools provide immense benefits, some challenges can impede the successful deployment of these tools. It's important to be aware of and manage:

1. **Data Privacy**: Ensure any AI tool follows all the necessary compliance regulations regarding data privacy.

2. **Integration**: The tool should be able to seamlessly integrate with the other systems you are currently using.

3. **Transparency**: Some AI tools provide very little insight into how they generate results or make decisions, which can be problematic for businesses.

AI tools are revolutionizing the operation of small businesses. By familiarizing yourself with these tools and understanding how they can help improve your business, you can take advantage of the AI revolution in the most beneficial way possible.

Chapter 8. AI Success Stories: Case Studies from Small Businesses

In the realm of small businesses, countless enterprises have proven that advanced technology isn't just the domain of big corporations. These AI success stories illustrate the power of integrating AI into a variety of business areas - from improving customer service and inventory management, to enhancing operational efficiency and developing unique products or services.

8.1. AI Case Study: StackAdapt

StackAdapt is a self-serve programmatic advertising platform based in Toronto. While managing hundreds of campaigns manually was a challenging task for this small business, extensive data analysis was even more laborious.

Using AI-based predictive modeling, StackAdapt developed a machine learning model to assess and predict the success of advertising campaigns based on factors such as ad frequency, ad size, form of engagement, and other key variables.

The outcome was a streamlined and efficient prediction system that reduced human resource expenditure, error rates, and improved campaign performance. In addition, it enabled them to handle a scalability of operations that would have been humanly impossible.

8.2. AI Case Study: Descartes Labs

Descartes Labs leveraged AI technology to solve critical environmental problems. This New Mexico-based geospatial analytics startup utilized machine learning algorithms and supercomputing technology to analyze satellite imagery. By sifting through massive data sets, they recognized trends and patterns relating to the Earth's resources, agriculture, and weather patterns.

This use of AI provided actionable insights into fundamental environmental issues, which they then offered to their clients, including energy, agriculture and government entities. The aim was not just improved efficiency, but also a contribution to global environmental sustainability.

8.3. AI Case Study: Kinetic

Kinetic, a New York-based wearables startup, used artificial intelligence to improve workplace safety. They developed a wearable device, akin to a smart watch, called REFLEX that uses machine learning to analyze body movements of industrial workers to identify high-risk postures.

The device sends real-time feedback to the user when it detects movement associated with a higher risk of injury. As a result, workers could adjust in real-time, reducing their risk of work-related injuries. This usage of AI technology not only made industrial workspaces safer, but it also helped companies reduce costs associated with injuries and worker compensation.

8.4. AI Case Study: Gong

A conversation analytics and salesforce training startup, Gong, turned to AI to help sales teams optimize their performance. Gong uses natural language processing and machine learning to record, transcribe, and analyze sales calls. This AI-driven approach enables it to recognize effective sales patterns and tactics, and also identify areas for improvement.

With the resulting insights, Gong enabled salespeople to adapt their strategies and improve performance based on previous successful experience. The streamlined process reduced training time and increased sales conversions, proving that even sales - an inherently "human" field, can be successfully enhanced with AI.

8.5. AI Case Study: Blue River Technology

California-based agriculture tech startup, Blue River Technology, deployed AI and computer vision for precise farming. They created 'See & Spray' robots that use machine learning to differentiate between crops and weeds. Only weeds are targeted and sprayed, significantly reducing the quantity of herbicides used, promoting cost efficiency, and environmental preservation.

These case studies highlight how different industries can, and have, successfully integrated AI into their businesses. The applications of AI are truly vast, as they can be adapted to fit a multitude of tasks. In the vision of these small businesses, AI isn't a far-off concept but a reality that is shaping and enhancing the present day world of business. AI is not beyond reach for small businesses, and with careful implementation, it can yield immense benefits.

Remember, in the world of AI, small businesses can think and act big. The key is to understand the potential of AI, identify the areas of your business that can be enhanced, and implement the right AI solution. Don't hesitate to start your AI journey today! The stories of these small businesses bear testament to the rewards that await.

Chapter 9. Staying Ahead: Navigating the AI Regulatory Landscape

Despite its seemingly complex veneer, understanding the regulatory landscape of AI is pivotal for any small business looking to harness its capabilities. AI regulations can fundamentally shape the way businesses operate in the digital era.

9.1. Understanding AI Regulations

AI regulations consist of rules and guidelines that control the usage and development of artificial intelligence technologies. These laws are enacted with the intention of protecting consumers, ensuring fairness, and maintaining transparency. But why is this important for small businesses? Compliance with AI regulations not only allows for ethical and sustainable business practices but also fosters trust with customers and partners.

9.2. The Development of AI Laws and Regulations

AI is a rapidly evolving technology, and as such, its regulations have been in constant flux. While the ongoing development of AI law can present challenges for businesses, it's essential to stay up-to-date to avoid potential pitfalls.

Initially, governing bodies had a 'laissez-faire' approach to AI regulation, allowing organizations to experiment and evolve their AI technologies. However, as AI started to permeate every facet of society, regulators recognized the need for a firmer hand. The

General Data Protection Regulation (GDPR) enacted by the European Union in 2018 served as a watershed moment in AI law. GDPR set precedence by framing rules around 'automated individual decision-making,' which lays the groundwork for AI regulation.

Now, most developed nations have AI regulations in place, with developing countries also recognizing the imperative need for AI laws.

9.3. AI Regulations: A Global Perspective

When utilizing AI solutions, small businesses are no longer confined to local or national boundaries; hence, it's crucial to be aware of the regulatory landscapes across the globe. In essence, the country where the data originated or where the AI application is used could dictate the regulation your business needs to follow.

For instance, in the European Union, the GDPR governs how businesses handle customer data. It mandates businesses to inform customers about AI decision-making and gives them a 'right to explanation.' Simultaneously, in the United States, there's currently no federal law regulating AI, though several states like California have passed privacy laws that indirectly touch on AI.

Asia offers a diverse landscape of AI regulation. Countries like Japan and Singapore have enacted comprehensive regulations that encourage AI innovation while protecting consumers. On the contrary, countries like China have stringent AI laws, especially around data and privacy.

9.4. Handling Data Responsibly: A Core Part of AI Regulation

A common thread linking most AI regulations is the responsible handling of data, which forms the core of numerous AI applications. Regulations about data privacy, protection, and transparency have critical implications for businesses using AI.

Transparency about data usage is becoming a standard requirement across nations. It's essential to clearly communicate with customers about what kind of data you're collecting, how it's being processed, and what AI systems will use it. Consent is a requisite before collecting any user data.

Data protection is another crucial element. Businesses need to ensure their security protocols are robust and can safeguard sensitive user data.

9.5. Adherence to Non-discrimination and Fairness

Fairness and non-discrimination in AI are principle areas of concern for regulators globally. AI systems learn from data, and if this data carries biases, the AI system will likely echo them, leading to discriminatory practices. To avoid such scenarios, businesses should ensure their AI systems are trained on diverse datasets and regularly checked for potential biases.

9.6. Navigating the Future of AI Regulation

Looking ahead, certain themes regarding the regulatory landscape of AI seem apparent. Regulations are shifting from a reactive approach to a proactive one, and regulatory bodies are keen to ensure that AI benefits everyone, with an emphasis on fairness and transparency.

Increased scrutiny around data and algorithms is to be expected. As such, your business model should incorporate strong data management practices and be prepared to divulge algorithm functionality if required.

In this era of technological evolution, AI regulation is the scaffolding that allows businesses to sustainably harness the power of AI. While at times challenging, navigating this landscape is not beyond the reach of small businesses – and with the right tools and knowledge, it can even become a competitive advantage. By keeping abreast of AI laws, exercising best practices for data management and ensuring ethical AI practices, you too can turn this new digital horizon to your benefit.

Chapter 10. Toward Futurism: Preparing Your Business for an AI-powered Future

As we hurtle forward into a future increasingly defined by artificial intelligence (AI), the businesses that will enjoy the most success are those that are prepared. But what does this preparation entail? Whether shaping your strategy or deciding how to invest, understanding and leveraging AI for the benefit of your venture is key.

10.1. Building an AI-Aware Culture

An AI-ready business begins with an AI-aware culture. This means fostering an environment where your team understands the groundbreaking potential of AI, and is comfortable engaging with it. Knowledge is essential. Encourage learning and understanding of AI; even if the intricacies remain the domain of AI experts, it is beneficial for everyone in the organization to grasp its core concepts and potential implications. Nurture an echo chamber where AI-related ideas, trends, and developments are regularly discussed and utilized.

Companies can sponsor AI workshops or continual education sessions. Online courses or pertinent technology news webpages can provide a wealth of accessible information. Remember that knowledge about AI isn't static; it's an ever-evolving field. Ensure that learning and development opportunities in your organization continue to adapt and evolve as well.

10.2. Integrating AI into Organizational Strategy

Integrating AI into organizational strategy offers another critical step toward preparation for an AI-driven future. Pinpoint areas where AI could enhance your operations, whether it's in customer service, data analysis, marketing, or elsewhere. Start by evaluating your organization's key performance indicators (KPIs) and critical areas needing improvement. Can an AI tool improve these metrics? If the answer is yes, then integration in that area could be well worth considering.

Moreover, integration isn't just about implementing AI tools, but about incorporating AI thinking into your strategy planning. Consider the future of your industry — are there upcoming trends or potential disruptions where AI could provide a competitive edge? Perhaps there are areas ripe for innovation where AI tools could help pioneer new offerings? Once identified, these should be factored into your strategic thinking.

10.3. Choosing the Right AI Tools

The next step in the process of AI democratization is choosing the right AI tools for your business. The selection should be aligned with two main factors: your business goals and your team's technical capabilities. Many vendors offer AI tools with different functionalities, such as machine learning, natural language processing, or predictive analytics. Choose the tools that align well with your outlined business needs.

Secondly, ensure your team is equipped to handle any AI tools you're considering. Some tools may require the expertise of data scientists, while others might be more user-friendly, needing only basic tech understanding. Gauge your team's skills and plan your AI tool selection accordingly.

10.4. Implementing AI Solutions

Implementation can be challenging. It requires careful planning, adequate budget allocation, and a commitment to continuous improvement. Start on a small scale, with one department or a single process. Once you have seen the benefits, scale up gradually.

A crucial element of implementation is testing. Your AI tools won't be perfect off the bat, so it's vital to test and tweak them for optimal performance. To benchmark success, set specific metrics based on your defined business goals. For example, if you have implemented AI in customer service, track measures like response time, customer satisfaction score and resolution rate. Remember, it's the return on investment that truly counts, not the complexity of the technology.

10.5. Preparing for Challenges

Unlocking the benefits of AI doesn't come without its challenges. Issues like data privacy, ethical considerations, and job displacement due to automation must be appropriately managed. Put in place measures to handle ethical and privacy issues transparently and responsibly. Communication is essential in mitigating the fear of replacement – it's not about replacing humans, but about augmenting human capabilities.

10.6. Reflecting on Progress

Finally, take a moment to reflect on your journey towards adopting AI. Have you been able to see a substantial improvement in your business metrics? Are your employees more engaged and less burdened with monotonous tasks? If the answer is 'yes', you are on the right path! Keep evolving, learning, and growing along with this remarkable technology.

Embracing artificial intelligence may initially seem daunting, but the potential rewards are monumental. By cultivating an AI-aware culture, integrating AI into your strategy, selecting appropriate AI tools, successfully implementing AI solutions, and preparing for the challenges it may pose, your organization is well on its way towards preparing for the AI-powered future!

Chapter 11. Kickstart Your AI Journey: A Practical Implementation Guide

Starting on the journey of integrating AI into your business operations may seem like a daunting task. No fear – with the right approach and a clear roadmap, you'll find it's not as complex as it seems. This chapter is your practical guide, step by step, to kickstarting and subsequently managing your AI journey effectively.

11.1. Understanding AI

Before implementing any technology into your business, understanding it is essential. AI is not a monolithic, unchanging technology. At the heart of AI are machine learning (ML) and artificial intelligence algorithms that gain insights from large amounts of data, learn from the input, and improve their performance over time.

AI can be as simple as a chatbot on your website answering FAQs, or as complex as predictive analytics changing the face of your supply chain management. Depending upon the nature of your business and your priorities, you can choose to implement AI in numerous ways.

11.2. Identifying Opportunities for AI

Once you've gained a basic understanding of AI, the next step is identifying where it can be deployed in your business. Start by examining your business processes and identifying the pain points - places where efficiency can be improved, costs reduced, or customer experience enhanced.

Sometimes, AI opportunities are not connected to fixing something broken but enhancing what's already working. AI could be used to provide predictive maintenance for your most beneficial processes, making them even more effective.

11.3. Developing a Strategy

Equipping yourself with an AI strategy can help align your AI initiatives with your business objectives. A well-crafted strategic plan should define:

- The purpose of integrating AI technologies
- The outcomes you're expecting
- Benchmarks for success
- Budget allocations

Another key part of this strategy is to identify the data needed to fuel your AI solutions. The proverb "garbage in, garbage out" holds true for AI. You need to ensure the data collected and fed into the AI models is of good quality, appropriately safeguarded, and ethically sourced.

11.4. Choosing the Right Tools and Partners

You don't need an in-house team of data scientists to leverage AI. Numerous SaaS (Software-as-a-Service) AI providers allow you to harness the power of AI without a significant initial investment. Evaluate these based on your budget, their performance ratings, and their relevance to your specific use case.

Selecting the right AI partner is just as important. You need an IT vendor who understands your business, the unique challenges you face, and how those can be overcome by AI.

11.5. Navigating Implementation

Implementation might seem like the biggest hurdle, but with proper planning, it doesn't have to be. Start small, preferably with one project where AI can make a significant impact. Once you've seen the benefits of this initial project, you can scale up the AI integration across your enterprise.

11.6. Continuous Learning and Improvement

AI is not a set-it-and-forget-it type of technology. Instead, it's crucial to maintain your AI systems by frequently retraining the AI models with fresh data. This ensures your AI models adapt to changes in the environment over time, thereby consistently providing accurate results.

Moreover, evaluating AI performance periodically aids in understanding what's working and what isn't. Through this iterative process of testing, learning, and improving, you're not just maintaining but enhancing your AI capabilities.

11.6.1. Embracing a Culture of AI

The adoption of AI should be seen as company-wide digital transformation. To successfully integrate AI into your business and derive maximum benefit, you need to foster a culture of embracing AI which may involve reskilling existing staff or recruiting new talent with the necessary skills.

11.7. Wrapping Up

To kickstart your AI journey, start by understanding what AI is and how it can help your business. Identify the opportunities, craft your strategy, choose the right tools, and partners, and you are ready for implementation.

Remember, diligence and continuous improvement are key to AI success. The road to AI integration might not be straight, but it is paved with immense potential. As long as you adapt and maintain a learning mindset, you're on the right track. Just remember to keep your overarching business objectives in sight, and be sure to upgrade your AI strategy as your business evolves.

Embrace AI, and you'll unlock new methods of driving business growth and staying competitive in today's data-driven world.